5 MODE

5 MODELS OF PRAYER

How to Pray Fervently Well and Expose yourself to the Holy Spirit Constantly

By:

Vitalis Essala

DEDICATION

To my lovely wife, Viviane D. Essala, who unwaveringly stands by my side. I love you, blessing!

CONTENT

FOREWORD

Friend, allow me to speak directly to you today. First, welcome to this program called 5 models of prayer. By reading this book, you will know how to pray fervently well and expose yourself to the Holy Spirit, constantly. My name is Vitalis Essala. With my wife, Viviane, we founded Winning Souls Ministries to equip families in their walk with the Lord. In fact, we help families, and the Church in extension, by opening the Word for them in prayer.

On a personal note, I have survived countless trials in this life. The Lord alone has seen me through all of them. One of those trials is cancer. Yes, I am a stage 4 cancer survivor.

My book, *The Belief Vaccine,* has more about that. The Creator of heaven and earth carried me on His wings to cross these seas with me. Therefore, my life is devoted entirely to Him to draw others to Him. Why tell you all of this? I am telling you all this for you to know that this book is not claiming any theological posits. Glad to know that theology will never bring anyone to heaven. The grace of God which is expressed by the life, the death, the resurrection of Christ, and the continued salvific action of the Holy Spirit will bring us to heaven. It is by faith that we know this. No human discourse can replace the grace of God. Therefore, as a wretched individual, conceived in sin, I have received the grace of God to appertain to the graciously saved ones that are eagerly awaiting the soon-coming of our Lord and Savior Jesus Christ. It is by that grace that one day, before I was diagnosed with cancer, I

2

received from God, in a way which is not necessary to explain, to write a book on prayer.

That book was to show an ordinary Christian to go back to what prayer was meant to be. That book, *Prayer As it Was Meant to Be*, is finished but, by God's choosing, has not been published yet. As a matter of fact, while praying about that book one day, the Holy Spirit stopped me sharply and impressed me to write a program that will be more practical than the first. He (the Holy Spirit) literally showed me the plan of this book you are holding in hand. I did not resist.

I reproduced His copy. This is it. It is not theology. It is no other human discipline. It is the language God speaks to humans through useless vessels like me. May you be blessed, abundantly, as you read it.

The devil tried me from all sides to stop this work. But the Lord delivered me for you to read it. Just as I did, it may be that you will receive vicious attacks of your very own. Fear not. But remember that Jesus is the winner of the cosmic great controversy. He will hold you on His shoulders. Keep the faith; practice your faith by praying after the models shown here. You will see a difference. The Lord will put a mark on you and separate you from the mockers.

As you already know, everything we do, we must do for the glory of God. Therefore, we must boost our action with prayer. Glad you are here. Let's get to the introduction of this program.

INTRODUCTION

Since the first prayer ever prayed on earth by man to this day, prayer has always been one of the most relevant ways to communicate with God. That first prayer was made by Cain. After he had murdered his brother, Abel, Cain faced the justice of God. God had just read him his sentence, and Cain found it to be too difficult to bear. He made a prayer in this manner:

"Surely You have driven me out this day from the face of the ground; I shall be hidden from

Your face; I shall be a fugitive and a vagabond on the earth, and it will happen that anyone who finds me will kill me." (Genesis 4: 14)

You may not see it as a prayer, but it was one. He put it in an affirmative way. In the language of his time, Cain clearly had formulated a prayer. And when you look at it, it seems as he had decided that this is what was going to happen, hoping that God would grant him his petition. But he could not decide on what those that found him would do. God was the only person to decide on that and approve it. He knew it and God knew it as well.

In fact, Cain made a request, which is to ask for something specific. He made a prayer to God. If per adventure God had kept silent, meaning God did not object to this request, it would have happened just as Cain had said in his prayer because even God's silence is an answer in itself. Now tell me, did God answer Cain's prayer or not?

God's Answer to Cain's Prayer

Yes, God did answer Cain's prayer. The Bible confirms it. Verse 15 of Genesis 4 says,

"*And the Lord said to him, 'Therefore, whoever kills Cain, vengeance shall be taken on him sevenfold.' And the Lord set a mark on Cain, lest anyone finding him should kill him.*"

Again, the statement that God used in answering Cain's prayer can surprise you. The reason some of you might be surprised is that we have set our mind to believing that an answered prayer is a "Yes" answer. But even our parents can teach us this. How many times have they answered us with a no? We cannot count.

I tell my kids that every time they go to someone to ask for something, they must expect at least two answers: yes or no. And they must make up their mind to live with the answer because they cannot make anyone say, "Yes!" All they can do is to ask. God answers every prayer either with a yes, a no, a wait, or a silence. Here He said no to Cain.

There is something interesting here to mention and keep in mind. Every time God answers a prayer, He seals His answer with His seal or a mark. God is an authority. When an authority sends out a correspondence, that authority marks the correspondence with their seal. This is not difficult to understand. Even you and I, we do it. When we send out a letter, a gift, or a package to someone, don't we sign it with our name? God made sure no one

8

mistook His words and He put a mark on Cain.

The Bible does not tell us what mark God put on Cain. Several tergiversations have been spread on this bible text, but it is not necessary to expand on that. All we can tell is that God sanctioned the conversation He had with Cain with a mark of protection on Cain.

It is possible that it was a visible sign and one everyone meeting Cain would recognize and understand. It is also possible that it was a spiritual sign. Nevertheless, the mind of men was not as beclouded with sin as it is in our time. Nowadays, our mind is hard to understand God's message and marks.

Cain was the second generation of humans descending directly from God. Anyone in his time, rebellious or obedient to

God, has a more advanced understanding of God's messages and could therefore easily recognize the mark on Cain and spare him. God did not want us to know what the sign was, and it is not important for us to want to know it.

This is a sad setting, but on a positive note, every time God answers our prayer, He seals the answer with a mark -- and anthropomorphically speaking -- to make sure that that answer gets delivered to us. Isn't that encouraging? Nothing can sidetrack God's answer to our prayer. So, why is it that we pray for years and we receive no sign? That doesn't apply to the divine realm. There is no such thing in heaven as praying and receiving no answer.

If we don't receive an answer to our prayer, it means we are distracted. Either we did not check our spiritual mailbox (no pun intended), or we did not appreciate the answer that we received, and we made an appeal.

Praying for a Wife

I once heard a story of a brother who prayed for a wife and asked God for a sign. He wanted a wife and had given God a sign that would show him who was going to be his wife. The sign was that he would go to church on a given day early and wait. The unmarried sister that would come first would be his wife. I think you see where I'm going with this. And a sister came but she was not who the brother expected. He ran back to God begging for an upgrade. Now if that brother goes for another year without being attached to someone, whose fault is it? Did God answer the brother's prayer or not? God always answers our prayers.

"Now it happened, when Jeremiah had stopped speaking to all the people all the words of the Lord their God, for which the Lord their God had sent him to them, all these words, that Azariah the son of Hoshaiah, Johanan the son of Kareah, and all the proud men spoke, saying to Jeremiah, 'You speak falsely! The Lord our God has not sent you to say, 'Do not go to Egypt to dwell there.' 3 But Baruch the son of Neriah has [a]set you against us, to deliver us into the hand of the Chaldeans, that they may put us to death or carry us away captive to Babylon.'" (Jeremiah 43: 1-3)

Here is a people who are being destroyed by the king of Babylon. A big portion of the population has been taken into captivity. The remnant staying in Jerusalem comes to the prophet and asks him to pray for them and asks for God's guidance. They

12

vehemently promise that they will do even as the Lord commands. Jeremiah prays and brings them word again. But since the answer he brings back does not validate their desire to go to Egypt, they decide to accuse Jeremiah of lying to destroy them. They not only refuse to follow the word of the Lord, but they also force the prophet to go to Egypt with them.

This is how we all are. We seek God's will to validate our desires. When that doesn't happen, we claim that He did not answer our prayer. Now, indeed, God does answer all our prayers. As you know, though, the purpose of this product is to show you five simple ways to approach prayer. It will help you always have something to say when you pray. Thus, you will develop a prayerful life. If you want to know how to listen to God and know His answer to our prayer, you may check with another product I wrote. It is called *How to Listen to God: 9 Channels you Must Use to Understand God's Will for your Life.*

***

Sometimes, we engage in prayer and in the middle of it we find ourselves struggling to find adequate words. Sometimes we just don't know what to say, where to start. In fact, we dread the idea of being chosen by the meeting coordinator to pray. If you have been in this situation, don't worry. You will never have that problem anymore if you carefully follow the principle I'm about to show you. I only have a word of caution before we start to develop our models.

How we Are Going to Proceed

I will give you the model, show you

how to apply it, and leave you in the Holy Spirit's care. Do not repeat my words in your prayers. They have no secret in them if you repeat them. In fact, I don't want you to practice prayer as a recitation or just something you have to do. Instead, a fulfilling Christian life is a life of intimacy with God.

When you are with your best friend, do you think that you have to be with them? Or would you repeat someone else's words to your friend and expect them to believe that you mean these words?

There are only two ways we can intimately connect with our Heavenly Father. We can only connect with Him through prayer and through His word. When you engage in prayer, do it as conversing with your Father and Friend who loves you unconditionally.

The second thing I want you to know is to study this process at least three times. Every time you study it, the Lord will help you learn a new thing. The Holy Spirit will teach you more skills than I. Ideally, go over the entire program once a month. Thank you for getting this program. Let us start with the first model now.

THE MODEL OF JESUS

On a normal day, I would start with other models and save the best for last. But Jesus is the Master. His voice should come first, and when we conclude with the last model, His guidance will also conclude. Having said that, let's see what the model of the Master is.

The Lord's Prayer

Jesus showed us His model of prayer in what theologians have called the Model Prayer or the Lord's Prayer. But let us precise that the prayer we are going to focus on here is more accurately the model prayer. The Lord's prayer is found in John 17. For popular purpose, we are going to use the term model prayer interchangeably with the Lord's prayer. We find the extended version of the model prayer in Matthew 6: 9-13. Here it is in the New King James Version.

"In this manner, therefore, pray:

Our Father in heaven,
Hallowed be Your name.
Your kingdom come.
Your will be done
On earth as it is in heaven.
Give us this day our daily bread.
And forgive us our debts,
As we forgive our debtors.
And do not lead us into temptation,
But deliver us from the evil one.
For Yours is the kingdom and the power and the glory forever. Amen."

I don't know if this is the exact order the Lord put it, but I believe every word He put in this model makes sense. Now why am I wondering if this is the order in which He put it? Because we, Christians, put confession of sin first, thinking that either it is just convenient to make peace with God before we ask for anything or God is a very grudgeful guy who would not hear us if we didn't soften His heart with confession. I know, there are many acronyms of prayer that don't put confession first, but generally we put confession first.

In this model prayer Jesus puts confession almost in the end. That shows me that it is important to confess, but God wants us to acknowledge Him first as the authority He is and know that He can grant us our requests. Now what does this model mean and how do we apply it? We will break it down section by section, and then in the end I will put the whole thing together in a prayer, just to show you how to apply it. Let's start by dissecting the model prayer.

The Model Prayer Dissected

Verse 9, Our Father in heaven, Hallowed be Your name.

There are two sections in this verse. The first is to recognize that God is our Father and He is in heaven. He is our Father; therefore, everyone has access to Him. Let no one lie to you that you should pay them to pray for you.

Your spiritual leaders have the authority to intercede for you, but that is different from telling you to stay put and do nothing while they pray for you. In fact, we can intercede for one another. We do not need to be a leader to pray for our sister or brother.

We all have access to our Father. That Father is in heaven. It means that He oversees every other realm. No one can dictate His decisions. That's good news because corruption is our way of functioning. God is influenced by no Interest Group. No congressional House has a say in His High-Court. His decisions are pure and exempt of any selfish motives.

The other section in this verse is *Hollowed be Your name*. When we come to God in prayer, we must know that His name is hallowed. Hallowed means holy. In Exodus 20: 7 He says,

"You shall not take the name of the Lord your God in vain, for the Lord will not

hold him guiltless who takes His name in vain."

So, when you come to God in prayer, know that you are talking to a Holy God whose name is to be hallowed. In a nutshell, when we come to God in prayer, we must worship Him.

In verse 10 there are three sections. The first is *Your kingdom come*. In Bible scenes, when a kingdom was powerful and undefeatable, the other kingdom came to the powerful and surrendered its authority to it. We see it in 1 Kings 20.

Ben-Hadad, the king of Assyria comes against Ahab, the king of Israel to war. But the Lord strengthens Ahab and he pursues and destroys the armies of Assyria along with the 32 kings Ben-Hadad had alliance with to defeat Israel. In verse 31, his servants come to Ben-

Hadad and advise him to go seek the clemency of Ahab and surrender to his authority.

When we come to God, we must agree to give up even our life to Him, so that He can become our King. Shouldn't we do this every day? Yes, we should. The second section in verse 10 is *Your will be done*.

When we come to God in prayer, Jesus is saying that we must accept whichever decision God will make. Remember when I said in the beginning that sometimes we don't value God's answer because we want something else? When we pray, we must agree to take God's decision.

The third part in this verse is *On earth as it is in heaven*. It doesn't make grammatical sense, but this phrase means God's authority and will must become ours even as it is in Heaven. We also need to understand that these words were a prophecy.

God's Kingdom will come on earth in due time. His Will, will be done on earth in due time. But that is another focus. Nevertheless, have you ever thought of this statement?

Jesus came from heaven. He knows how it is in heaven. The will of God is done in perfection in heaven. What God says is done. What He says is done as He said it. It is done when He said it should be done. No one questions God. Why does no one question God's decisions in heaven? Because heavenly beings acknowledge the wisdom of our Father, and they know that His decisions are for the good and happiness of His children. So, Jesus is not naïve when He says that we should pray for the will of God to be done on earth as it is

24

in heaven.

Jesus knows what He's talking about. He knows our limits. He knows the limits of our will. If He is telling us to do the will of God on earth as it is done in heaven, Jesus knows that we can do it if we are willing. Isn't that impressive? The Holy Spirit can help us know and do the will of God without questioning it.

Coming back to Matthew 6, let's look at verse 11, we see one focus: *Give us this day our daily bread.* This is the bucket where you put all your cares, concerns, and requests. The first two verses were on worshiping God. Now that you have acknowledged God as everything, the focus is on you.

Do you need anything? This is where you express it. Verse 12 has two focuses: the first is, *And forgive us our debts.*

We are sinners. Isaiah 64: 6 says that

"...all our

righteousnesses are like filthy rags..."

But God is holy and pure. We cannot come to Him in our sinful nature and stand. Our sins are a debt to pay. They are the reason Satan accuses us all the time. God is righteous. He put a principle in place – confession of sins – through which He will exonerate us and free us from the debt of sin. Therefore, we must ask for forgiveness, so that He will cleanse our sins away. This is whether we came to worship God, to praise Him, to make a request, or to intercede for someone. The second section of this verse is, *As we forgive our debtors.*

This implies that we are forgiving. If we cannot forgive, why should God forgive us? Jesus is telling us that we must extend our mercy on others as God has extended His mercy on us.

When we come to God, we must free our heart from any grudge and forgive our brothers in our heart. When you continue the reading of this chapter, verse 14 will tell you that if we don't forgive our brothers and sisters, our heavenly Father will not forgive us either.

Verse 13 has three sections. Two on us through God, and the last on God again. The first section is, *And do not lead us into temptation.*

We must pray for God to preserve us from getting trapped into temptation. It means that temptation will not depart from us until the day we die, or when Jesus comes back. 1 Peter 5: 8 says that *"[our] adversary the devil walks about like a roaring lion, seeking whom he may devour."*

Falling into temptation would be as falling into the lion's mouth. Now we cannot avoid the lion's mouth on our own. God is He who can help us escape the devil's snares. "Without me you can do nothing," says Jesus (John 15: 5.)

God does not force Himself into anyone's business. He helps those that give Him permission. When we pray God to lead us not into temptation, He sends His holy angels to guide our steps and keep us. The Psalmist says this prayer:

"Direct my steps by Your word, and let no iniquity have dominion over me." (Psalms 119: 133)

In the same book, (91: 11), that the devil misquoted to Jesus, the Bible says:

"For He shall give His angels charge over you, to keep you in all your ways."

"All your ways" here is as you follow God's guidance. You must make a conscious effort to follow the voice of God and then His angels will assist you to stay on course. If you decide to err, angels will not assist you; they may urge you by placing the consequences to incur before you, but you are the one to decide.

The second section of verse 13 is, *But deliver us from the evil one.* Not only should God prevent us from falling into temptation, and even when we fall into temptation, we must pray for the same God to pull us out of the trap.

When we fall into temptation, we are in

29

Satan's mercy. We have seen devout Christians falling and never coming back to Christ. That is when you fall, and you decide to not seek for forgiveness. You rather entertain your pride.

The devil enjoys it when someone grows in pride. He, the devil, will take such a person away from the presence of God. Satan is not more powerful than the angels of God. But your protecting angels have a direct order to work with your will. If you choose sin, Satan has your permission to torment you. If you strive against sin, the angels of God will assist you overcome. We must pray to get out of the devil's hands when we fall in them.

The last section says, *For Yours is the kingdom and the power and the glory forever. Amen.* We go back to worshipping God. We can see why this model is the model prayer. Now let me put the whole thing together in a prayer that respects this order. I am going to use the context of a family. It is not my family; it is a fictitious family of three.

Practical Prayer

Our Father in heaven, I bless your name for giving me access to You. I am not worthy of your Holy Place, but by your unfailing love, I can address the God of gods and Lord of lords. I thank you Father because I have access to your counsel. The same is true for my wife VIVI, and my daughter Marie. They also have access to You only by your love for us.

Hallowed be Your name, O Lord! Your name is above all names, O God. In your name every tongue should confess that Jesus Christ is Lord, to the glory of God the Father. Every knee shall bow to You, and every tongue shall confess to God. Jesus, I confess that you are Lord, and as I live, I will teach my family to revere your name.

Your kingdom come. Be my King Jehovah, be my King. Show me how to be a loving leader to my family and to all the flocks you will give me in life, whether in the church or in secular life. I surrender my authority to You. You must increase, Jesus, but I must decrease. I surrender my intelligence, belongings, and self to You. Be my King now and forever.

Your will be done. What you say is what I will do, Father. Holy Spirit, I will follow your guidance. When you ask me to go up, I will go, and when you tell me to forebear, I will wait on You. I don't even know my whereabouts, Holy Ghost, show me around and let me follow you. Remember, I am a stranger on the earth; Do not hide Your commandments from me. Please let your will be done in my life and in Vivi's as well as in Marie's. We need to know your commandments. Please do not hide them from us. Your will be done on earth as it is in heaven, Lord. I pray that I will do your will and only your will in my family, Father. I also present your servant, my wife to you. Please assist her in her spiritual journey to know and do your will. The same for Marie, my daughter. She is so young, and please build her small faith in your will.

God, we have so much on our plate that only your grace can help us. Since you said we should ask of you, God, Give us this day our daily bread. My boss expects more of me that I can offer. Father, maybe I am able to offer that much and even more. Now whether I am able to or not, please give me your wisdom and help me hone my skills to do my job with excellence. Additionally, my wife is pursuing a training in coding.

She was complaining last night that she is behind in her assignments. Please teach her wise strategies to apply to get ahead of the schedule. Again, my daughter is young. She is taking her first steps to school. Please protect her. The time is evil, Jesus. Children are being slaughtered daily in schools. Please protect my little Marie.

God, brother Ariel lost his job of fourteen years. You promised that we should call on you, and you will answer us, and show us great and mighty things, which we do not know. This is the time to show these things. Help brother Ariel as he works through this phase of job hunting. Help him find work he loves and that he will set him time aside to worship you still.

We know, Lord, we do not deserve your mercies. But in Christ Jesus we have received all things and access. Forgive us our debts, O Lord. We are so loaded with pride, and anger, and disobedience. Cleanse us from our sinful ways of immorality and hatred.

Please help us forgive our debtors also. Our heart has wandered away so far away from you that we have forgotten how much you forgive us. We hold our brethren captive in our heart, Father. I pray that you will help us learn to forgive.

Moreover, do not lead us into temptation. Our accuser, the devil, is roaring all around us. Be close by us, dear Jesus. We need you. Give us wisdom to learn and know your word so that we will resist the devil when he comes.

Finally, God, deliver us from the evil one. Your word says that the angel of the Lord encamps all around those who fear Him, and delivers them. Let it be true for me, Father. Let it be true for my wife, and let it be true for Marie. Not only that, let your angel encamp all around the families of my church. We have been losing many members of our families lately. Please protect us going forward. Even though death is a foreseeable passage to humankind, Lord, some people die before their time because of the choices they make for their lives. For those I pray. Give them wisdom to make wise choices and live to the fullness of their set times.

For Yours is the kingdom and the power and the glory forever. Amen.

THE MODEL OF THE FIVE AREAS OF LIFE

You can find multiple areas of life. But they all hinge around five main ones. These five areas are: spiritual, health, emotional/sentimental, financial, and social. These five areas define our life. Basing prayer on or around them will help you remember the topics you would forget if you didn't have a prayer book, which is one of the best prayer guides a Christian should have. Even when you do not have a prayer book where you record your prayer topics, these models will help you touch on everything and have enough words to express yourself before God. Let's see how this model of the five areas of life can be used.

The Spiritual Area

The first area is spiritual. I don't agree that one can be spiritual but not a believer. You do not have to espouse my view, but that's what I know. We are a believer and therefore we have a spiritual meaning of life or we are not, and we only exist. Nevertheless, let's not direct our focus elsewhere.

When you pray using the spiritual area of life, this is where you go over your relationship with God, your family's relationship with God, and anyone you want to pray for. Why must we go over these relationships with God at this moment? Because *"God is Spirit, and those who worship Him must worship in spirit and truth."* That's what Jesus Himself told the Samaritan woman at the well in John 4: 24.

You cannot get to God in flesh. And God reaches us in spirit when He wants to reach us. He does not speak to our flesh. He talks to our spirit, which is symbolized by our mind. Some schools will speak about the heart. The mind here or heart is not the organ of the brain or the blood pump. It is the spiritual dimension of humanity.

Speaking to the Thessalonians, Paul says this blessing:

"Now may the God of peace Himself sanctify you completely; and may your whole

spirit, soul, and body be preserved blameless at the coming of our Lord Jesus Christ." (1 Thessalonians 5: 23)

Jesus said that the true worshipers worship in spirit. That means that we use our heart and mind for pure purposes knowing that they are special spots that God influences when He wants to reach us.

Proverbs 4:23 says:

"Keep your heart with all diligence,

For out of it spring the issues of life."

Our heart is where the source of our life springs from indeed. And who is the source of that life? God is! A healthy heart can beat for a hundred years without replacement and without recharging the battery. Who charges the battery of our heart? God does!

Therefore, we ought to take good care of that heart because it has a specific connection with God and our life. Not only that, because this is a mechanical connection with God, but our heart makes our decisions and most of our choices. These decisions and choices can bring us up to heaven or bring us down to hell. In a nutshell then, our spiritual self or spiritual area of life is what determines our relationship with God.

When we pray concerning our spiritual self, we must go back to the Lord's model of prayer. We must worship God first. Worship is spiritual, that's what we've been saying all along. After worshiping, we must tell God where our relationship with Him is. If we wrecked our relationship with Him, we must state it. The next part is confession.

We must confess for ourselves, our

family, and for whomever we are praying. The Bible says:

"It may be that my sons have sinned and cursed God in their hearts. Thus Job did regularly." (Job 1: 5.)

Job prayed and confessed for his sons regularly. We must also confess for our children. After our confession, we may now proceed to make spiritual requests before we move to our health area. I will show you how to do so when we get to the application of this model. For now, let's study the health area.

The Health Area

"The Spirit of the Lord is upon Me, Because He has anointed Me To preach the gospel to the poor; He has sent Me to heal the brokenhearted, To proclaim liberty to the captives

And recovery of sight to the blind, To set at liberty those who are oppressed."

This is the gospel of Luke 4: 18. Jesus is laying out His mission statement. And although you can have a spiritual interpretation of this passage, the brokenhearted, the captive, the blind, and the oppressed will tell you that it has influence on physical and emotional health. What I'm trying to say is that a sick person cannot function well. We need good health.

Therefore, when you get to the health area, pray for your health, your family's health, and the health of whomever comes up in your prayer.

"By His stripes we are healed."

Jesus will heal us if we pray. One of the gifts and promises that Jesus gave us was to pray for the sick so that they will recover. "They will lay hands on the sick, and they will recover," He said speaking about us.

Whether you are praying specifically for a sick person or just praying in general, worship God first and then move on to whatever subject you have. The passage of Mark 16 I just mentioned is to encourage us that we received mandate, we received permission from the Lord that we can pray for the sick. Even if we are not close to them to lay hands on them, we can still pray. We must pray for health and healing because of sin.

Every time someone has sinned in the Bible, or God has mentioned prayer, He accompanied forgiveness with healing. We have a few instances where that does appear. One of them is in 2 Chronicles chapter 7: 14.

"If My people who are called by My name will humble themselves, and pray and seek My face, and turn from their wicked ways, then I will hear from heaven, and will forgive their sin and heal their land."

Sin brings sterility. It brings sickness. Sterility is not a natural occurrence. There has to be a dysfunction or distracting factor for sterility to take place. That factor is what God addresses when He forgives and healing proceeds thereof.

When you pray for health and healing, pray for forgiveness first. That does not mean that all sickness proceeds out of sin. But we are in a sinful nature. We are sick because sin entered the world. Without sin there will be no sickness. Even though you will posit that Jesus was talking about the spiritual blindness, He healed physical blindness, didn't He? Those

45

sick and poor were despised by the members of the Sanhedrin in the time of Christ. He came to announce a year of liberation to those poor.

We need forgiveness even when we do not feel guilty of anything. Pray for your health and healing as well as for the persons you are presenting to God.

"So Abraham prayed to God; and God healed Abimelech, his wife, and his female servants. Then they bore children; for the Lord had closed up all the wombs of the house of Abimelech because of Sarah, Abraham's wife." (Genesis 20: 17, 18)

As you can see, sin brings sterility. Forgiveness brings healing. When you pray for healing, extend it to the real cause of sickness which is sin.

In this illustration, Abimelech did not

sin in the act but had sinned in the intention. God sees sin before the action takes place. Now we know that much sorrows follows us because our mind is not clean. Only the blood of Jesus can cleanse us. Pray for health and healing with that in mind. Health influences how we feel and how we relate to others.

The Emotional/Sentimental Area

We all have the need to love, be loved, and belong. In Maslow's hierarchy of needs, love and belonging appears on the third level of needs. Let me say something that will shock some of you.

If you see a homeless person, chances are that person does not have that love connection with a strong base. Love is known to be the strongest emotion because of its constructive power. A destroyed life is a life that did not relate or did not find how to convey their love and relate to others' love.

God is love. He wants us to relate to others by and with love. The second greatest commandment is to love your neighbor as yourself. When a lawyer came to test Jesus, he asked about the greatest commandment in the law. Jesus answered and moved on to address the real issue of all humankind.

"And the second is like it: 'You shall love your neighbor as yourself.'" (Matthew 22: 39)

The greatest commandment is to Love the Lord. Jesus addressed the biggest issue of humankind. That biggest issue is the lack of love for one another. He even gave His last will by saying that the world will know you by

48

your love. Churches must focus more on love.

Our preaching and teaching must show love, teach love, and promote love. We must show the love of God and present God as our loving Father instead of only presenting God as a judge. He is a judge but does not delight in the death of a sinner. We must also teach and promote love for one another.

If Christians loved one another Christlike, church members would have a more fulfilling life. They would support one another to find better jobs, they would recommend one another for grad education, jobs, and general purposes. Poverty, resentment, and misery would not overwhelm church members the way it does right now.

I will insist that churches must focus on love for God. God is first, and God is last.

What do we love the most?

"No one can serve two masters; for either he will hate the one and love the other, or else he will be loyal to one and despise the other. You cannot serve God and mammon." (Matthew 6: 24.)

Jesus did not let us make any confusion. You love who you serve, and you serve who you love. When our love for our spouse or child, or job, or sports surpasses our love for the Lord God, in the spiritual realm, we are an idolater. We are serving another master. If our emotions are saturated with anger, drugs, sexual immorality to the point of being addicted to those things, our love for God is dim if it ever exists.

So, when you pray for love and sentimental needs, don't just pray for your spouse to love you more or for you to love them more. It's not just about espousal love. Love is so much more than erotic feelings. It is filial love (love for a parent or sibling) and it is agape or charitable love for a person or for God. That is love which is praiseworthy, and that is the love that should be the object of our thoughts, and that is love we must pray for concerning ourselves, our family members, and our fellow humans.

"Finally, brethren, whatever things are true, whatever things are noble, whatever things are just, whatever things are pure, whatever things are lovely, whatever things are of good report, if there is any virtue and if there is anything praiseworthy – meditate on these things." (Philippians 4: 8)

This is what we should work for instead of just working for money.

The Financial Area

The second part of Ecclesiastes 10: 19 says that "*money answers everything.*" It is not a bad thing then to seek and save money. It is not a bad thing to have money, lots of money. And that is going to be all for my theology on money today. The focus is prayer. God's desire is that we prosper. Prospering means taking care of ourselves and our family, at the bare minimum.

Whenever we lack money or financial resources to pay for our shelter such as rent or mortgage, to place food on the table, to clothe ourselves, to provide decent means of transportation to our family, to receive proper health care, and to entertain ourselves, we are not prospering. This is not spiritual. It is reality.

When you pray, pray for enough financial resources in your family. If you are the head of the household, you need to double on your prayers about this. Your family depends on you. You should depend on God. If you are a member of the family, pray for financial blessing in your family. Many problems will not happen or will be easily minimized if you have enough resources with which to live. But if your resources are scarce, your problems will increase. We should pray for financial resources in the family and the church, so that we can take care of our families.

What does Paul say to Timothy?

"But if anyone does not provide for his own, and especially for those of his household, he has denied the faith and is worse than an unbeliever." (1 Timothy 5: 8)

Plain and simple. Now, there are extenuating circumstances. If you do everything in your power and things are still out of your control, you can be an exception. But it cannot go on indeterminately. There's got to be a stop somewhere even if it means seeking help.

God has our best interest in mind. He said:

"Ask, and it will be given to you; seek, and you will find; knock, and it will be opened to you."

When you pray for financial resources, remind Him of that promise. Also, ask Him to teach you how to ask. If you are applying for different positions and you haven't heard back from those employers, ask God. He will tell you what's going on. He answers us in many ways in case you wonder how He's going to tell you. He can put a thought in your mind to explore, or have someone provide you with a great resource, or He can lead you toward a career coach that will fine-tune your resume and help you better present your skills. God uses multiple ways to talk to us.

Another thing I believe is that churches must invest in personal development for their members. Churches must teach their members how to sharpen their skills and how to present them to potential employers and put in place a non-profit staffing department for their members. Some churches do, and they do it very well. All churches must follow the lead.

Likewise, churches must teach their members how to be good stewards of their money and financial resources. That is taking care of your members holistically, or body, soul, and spirit. The more independent the members are financially, the stronger the church will be.

I am not talking about the gospel that doesn't point people to Christ but to worldly materials. I am talking about the gospel that only points people to Christ and never to their earthly responsibilities.

Just to close this topic in good terms, please trust me that I understand that not everyone is going to have much money. Some will get materialistic means more than others. Those that have less should not feel left out by the Lord. Everything we receive is His and for His glory. So, whether you have much or not, glorify God for what you have.

We are social beings, and we are bound to the coercive power of social responsibilities. We must function socially so that our spiritual can be balanced.

The Social Area

"I do not pray that You should take them out of the world, but that You should keep them from the evil one." (John 17: 15)

This is Jesus praying to the Father before His departure from the world. He did not ask that we be removed from the world. We are still living on earth. We must go to school, rent or mortgage a house, seek transportation, pursue a career. These are coercive necessities we must meet. This area is where you pray for what does not necessarily fit in the first four areas.

If you have a frightening boss, this is where you introduce them to God in your prayer. If you do not know how to train your child to behave formally in society, this is where you pray for it. If you want to get to Ivy League schools, this is where you pray for it. I am not alleging that only those that go to elite schools are better off or get the best instruction. It is a simple example. If you are planning to leave the corporate world and start your business, this is where you pray for it.

In 1 Corinthians 12: 31, we read:

"...earnestly desire the best gifts."

In current language Paul meant to say, "Dream big!" It is fine to dream big, to look for ways to invent a cure for cancer, to reverse sickle cell anemia, to perform noninvasive surgery. It is fine to want to write a book, to become a public speaker, or to buy a bigger house. If you do it with the means that God gives you through your efforts, that is fine.

And this is where you pray for it.

"And Jabez called on the God of Israel saying, 'Oh, that You would bless me indeed, and enlarge my territory, that Your hand would be with me, and that You would keep me from evil, that I may not cause pain!' So God granted him what he requested." (1 Chronicles 4: 10)

In Bible time, names had meanings. Either they described what was happening at birth or the name predicted the child's future. The best illustration of the name of a child predicting its future is Jesus.

"She will bring forth a Son, and you shall call His name Jesus, for He will save His people from their sins." (Matthew 1: 21)

The angel came to Joseph and explained to him why his wife was with child. And the same angel gave him the name he should call

59

the child that his wife would bring forth. So, Jesus means Savior as well as Noah. The same principle seems to apply with Jabez.

I didn't find any specific elaborate information about the birth of Jabez. But with our knowledge of the Bible, we know that his name means distress or pain because either his mother had too much physical or emotional pain while bearing him or she predicted a distressful future for her child. Either way, Jabez prayed and asked for a better ending of his life. The Bible says that Jabez was more honorable than his brothers.

If you know someone whose life is meaningless or sifted all around, this is where you present them to God. Although Jabez's story has spiritual connotations, his social becoming was at stake, which is why we put it here. Every time an area does not fit the rest of the four areas, put it in this social area. That doesn't mean that this area is a dumpster area. A better way to say this is that if something has social impact on you, put it here. Here we are done with theory. Let's now move on to the practical application of it.

Practical Prayer

Blessed and everlasting Father, thank you for the gift of life. Lord, I thank you for giving me the opportunity to be in front of you today. Lord, I haven't been praying that much lately, and my spiritual connection with You is rusty. Only you can make it whole again, Father. Please draw me closer to You, O Lord. Help me love your word again, study it, share it, and live it. I pray that You will help me pray without ceasing. Apply this request on my wife Vivi too, Father as well as on our daughter Marie.

Help us love you more than anything else and help us practice fraternal fellowship. This way, our heart will fully turn to You. Indeed, your word says:

"For the eyes of the Lord run to and fro throughout the whole earth, to show Himself strong on behalf of those whose heart is loyal to Him."

Likewise, Lord, I pray that our health be in your Hands. Chronic and incurable diseases sweep the land right in these days. Please protect us from them. We know that we are still in a broken flesh. It is subject to weakness. But keep us against terrible sicknesses. You promised in your word saying:

"The Lord will take away from you all sickness, and will afflict you with none of the terrible diseases of Egypt which you have

62

known."

Another area the devil influences in our lives, Lord, is fellowship with each other. In our church couples need you, Lord. We want to enjoy our marriages, Father, because they are a gift you gave us. Please help us love our spouses like ourselves. You designed married people to become one in mind, in spirit, and in everything. But the trials of this world tear us apart. The same is true among brethren. Church members don't practice love as Jesus recommended us. I pray for love in the church. I pray for love in families. I pray that we love you more.

We are spoiled in despair. We earn little and the wind blows away all our earnings. Lord, part of it is because we are no more faithful in our tithing. Your word is clear that if we tithe, you will open for us the windows of heaven and pour out for us such blessing that there will not be room enough to receive it. But Lord, Your church has become one of the most miserable places where members are oppressed from all sides and prostrated.

We are jobless. Our endeavors end up in meager returns. Lord, teach us to trust you and bless your people financially and materialistically. Father, my family needs a new car. My car broke down last week again. I have to rent a car in such financially tight moments. Guide us as we look for a new vehicle. My wife is also pursuing her degree in criminal justice. She has been complaining of too many assignments in forensic psychology. Please help her organize her priorities and find a strategic method of learning. Father I ask you this in Jesus name. Amen.

THE MODEL OF THE SEVEN CAPITAL SINS

There is a certain belief that there are seven capital sins. They are pride, greed/selfishness, lust or sexual immorality, envy, gluttony, wrath, and sloth. I don't have a biblical base for categorizing these sins as the deadly sins. Every sin is equally deadly. This list of seven sins came from the writings of Monk Evagrius Ponticus, in the Fourth Century. He listed eight deadly sins. Later, they were brought down to seven. Once more, there are as many deadly sins as there are thoughts.

If you can count your thoughts, multiply the number by your actions, add your words, and multiply that by your omissions, then the final number is the number of deadly sins. That is my estimation. But if there are innumerable sins, why base prayer on a model of seven? Because these seven capture important aspects of life from where sins grow.

These aspects are lustful appetite such as gluttony, fornication, and avarice. Irascibility such as wrath. Mind corruption such vainglory, sorrow, pride, and discouragement. We could give an extended talk on each of these aspects, but our focus is prayer. So, let's elaborate this model of the seven deadly sins from the standpoint of prayer.

Pride

Pride, in the negative connotation, is the vicious expression of self, implying personal superiority and value over anyone else. Pride is one of the primary sins Satan committed in heaven when he was still standing before God. He estimated himself more important than God the Father, God the Son, and God the Holy Spirit, and he wanted to sit above the trinity.

The Bible bears this testimony:

"For you have said in your heart: 'I will ascend into heaven, I will exalt my throne above the stars of God; I will also sit on the mount of the congregation On the farthest sides of the north; I will ascend above the heights of the clouds, I will be like the Most High.'" (Isaiah 14: 13, 14)

If this is not pride, what else is? Do we think we deserve more than our boss sometimes, or that we are better than our pastor, or that we know better than God who created us? Are we proud then? Not necessarily because, of course, we can have knowledge on some topics more than our pastor, and they won't be sad about that. But how we express our knowledge can hint out pride. Most of us struggle with negative pride.

Let's just divert for a moment. Is there really a positive pride? The term, "I'm proud of you!" presumes that there is a positive pride, but proud is proud and it is sin. If you don't agree, let's face it. Can you tell someone, "I'm liar of you?" or "I'm murderer of you?" or "I'm thief of you?" Oh, it wouldn't make any sense? Then "I'm proud of you!" makes no sense except to advance sin.

Here is another expression: "We pride ourselves on..." or "We take pride in..." Both mean that one provides pioneering stand in something. But is there not a sinless way of saying the same thing? How about we distinguish ourselves in... or we stand out from the crowd on...? We cannot say, "We murder ourselves in..." or "We steal ourselves in..." or "We lie ourselves in..." It would just make you laugh, right? My point exactly. Pride is sin, and we must pray for victory over pride. Why?

A proud person is blinded by their pride. They don't see their limitations. Who does not know or see their limitations and shortcomings is open to despicable mistakes. Not only that, that person is not contrite. If they can't make mistakes why would they repent even if you proved them wrong? And when someone is not repentant, they are a good candidate for hell. They are close to blaspheming the Holy Spirit. You see, we talk about blaspheming the Holy Spirit as the unforgivable sin. But one does not just go straight to blaspheming. They usually start with small things. From small thing to small thing, they end up adding up layer upon layer. Finally, their conscience becomes numb. And the worst arrives. That is why we should pray for victory over pride. When you sin, what happens is that the Holy Spirit convinces you. To continue being under God's protection, you must repent. If your pride will keep you from repenting, then you will continue in your downward track of self-centeredness.

Greed/Selfishness

Greed is the desire to acquire more than

needed even in the expense of others that need it. I coupled greed with selfishness because selfishness is what triggers greed. A greedy or selfish person forgets or does not care that there are other people around them. They only see themselves. They can step on others just to get what they want. In fact, a greedy person is specialized in stepping on others to get ahead. That is in direct opposition with what God recommends.

Romans 12: 10 says:

"Be kindly affectionate to one another with brotherly love, in honor giving preference to one another."

The Word of God promotes self-denial. Jesus never showed a sign to prove anything or to elevate Himself. All He did was to relieve human condition and vindicate the Father. But a selfish and greedy person shows no affection, they honor themselves, and give preference to themselves only.

If I were to say corporate greed, almost everyone reading this would say, "yes!" But what is corporate? Corporate is a congregation of individuals. We know, when we speak of corporate greed we speak of the top officials that make 200 times the salary of their employees. But greed is not just found in the Corporate World. In our own family greed exists. It just takes multiple forms. For those of us who use social media, we show greed and selfishness daily.

When we post something, we want everyone in our circle to like it and share it to their circles. But we never like anything else, we never share anyone's post because we think their posts don't matter. That is selfishness.

When we were growing up, our parents taught us how to be selfless in this manner. If they had a cake to share, they would give it to the oldest of our siblings. It never was me. The oldest would divide it according to the number of the children. And then they would step aside. The other siblings would come, one by one, to take their share, beginning by the youngest, which was always me this time. The oldest divided the meal, and took their share last. That way, the oldest sibling made sure all the pieces were equal even when they lusted for more. We must pray for victory over greed.

Lust or Sexual Immorality

Lust is always associated with sexual immorality; it is an exaggerated desire to get something. In fact, lust is craving. One can crave for power, for sex, or for food. Lust goes beyond wanting. It has a locking mechanism that creates the sinful environment that produces all kinds of misconduct.

"For all that is in the world – the lust of the flesh, the lust of the eyes, and the pride of life – is not of the Father but is of the world." (1 John 2: 16)

This passage is telling us that the flesh does not want anything to its just measure. It wants it to overflow itself with the object of its desire. Now we know that everything taken or done to excess is dangerous even when its first nature is harmless.

Sugar is a good thing. But take too much of it, and you stand a chance to become either obese or diabetic. Salt is good also, but take too much of it, and you run the risk of developing many a condition.

"Excess sodium increases blood

pressure because it holds excess fluid in the body, and that creates an added burden on the heart. Too much sodium will increase your risk of stroke, heart failure, osteoporosis, stomach cancer and kidney disease. And, 1 in 3 Americans will develop high blood pressure in their lifetime." (Livestrong, 2012)

The flesh lusts after the things of the world and we start leaving God aside to pursue after the pleasures and belongings of this world.

We need to pray for victory over lust. If we were ever above any sin, that sin would not be lust. Our flesh is so intense in its desires that we need God's taming to keep it in check. When you pray, pray for lust in your life, in your family's, and in the lives of the people you pray for. The farther we go from intense prayer, the lustier our flesh gets because we take our eyes off the Lord. Let me say it differently.

We must pray intensely, or else our flesh will become more lustful for our destruction.

"But lusted exceedingly in the wilderness, And tested God in the desert."

This is the psalmist speaking about the Israelites who forgot God's abundant power and love in the desert and lusted after the things of the world. It doesn't take too much effort to start drifting away from God. It takes one day of not praying at a time. Lust is as strong as envy. Who lusts will develop envy.

Envy

Envy is desiring to possess what the

other person has or desiring that the other person lacked it. Either way, it is sin. The Lord is clear in His commandment.

"You shall not covet your neighbor's house; you shall not covet your neighbor's wife, nor his male servant, nor his female servant, nor his ox, nor his donkey, nor anything that is your neighbor's." (Exodus 20: 17)

Covetousness is the beginning of envy. Or they are twins. You can't envy without coveting and vice versa. Envy seems to be stronger because it can result in murder or provocative behaviors in its intense capacity.

"For he had possessions of flocks and possessions of herds and a great number of servants. So, the Philistines envied him." (Genesis 26: 14)

Isaac was living in the land of Abimelech, the king of the Philistines. He had great possessions. They envied him. Their envy was so intense that they went up to filling the wells Abraham had dug in the past.

Our envy may not cause us to do harm to somebody, but it may cause us to omit to do good to somebody, which is the same thing.

"Therefore, to him who   knows to do   good and does not do it, to him it is sin." (James 4: 17)

That's right; envy can blind our drive to do good, even to the person who is entitled to a service just because we don't want them to enjoy the benefit of that service. If you are sitting right there at that desk to serve your City, and by envy you deny someone a service to which he or she is entitled, that is sin.

It would be fair to state that envy engendered pride in Heaven and murder on earth. In Heaven, Satan envied Christ who, he thought was no different from himself. The Father had made it clear that Christ was to be honored and revered by all the heavenly beings and all the worlds. He was to be as the Father and all the honor due to the Father was due to the Son just as equally. Lucifer then glorious and powerful but holding a position lower than Michael was not invited when God held His High Council concerning the multiple worlds of the Universe. He then was full of envy and conceived pride. The result was his expulsion from Heaven along with his followers.

On earth, Cain envied his brother Abel because his offering was not accepted of God. This second generation of humans had the privilege to hear the story of salvation and Man's fall from Adam himself. They had the privilege of receiving the constant visits of holy angels guiding them in their ways. Cain well knew that God had cursed the ground because of sin. He knew that God required the sacrifice of animals and not of the fruit of the ground. The sacrifice of animals was thus preferred of God because He wanted every generation of Men to foresee the perfect sacrifice of the Lamb of God in Christ. No sap of the tree was to atone for the human race. The blood of Christ was the sacrifice prepared for us before the world began. But Cain willingly denied the privilege to set his heart on the sacrifice of Christ. Even after his sacrifice was not honored angels advised him on the right course to take. But sadly, the Bible says,

"So the Lord said to Cain, 'Why are you angry? And why has your countenance fallen? 7 If you do well, will you not be accepted? And if you do

not do well, sin lies at the door. And its desire is [d]for you, but you should rule over it.'" (Genesis 4: 6, 7)

God gave Cain the strength to overcome the sin of his heart, but envy got the best of him. He refused to heed the voice of the angel of God and murdered his brother. Envy is not a good feeling to nurture. We must pray for victory over envy also.

Gluttony

"When you sit down to eat with a ruler, Consider carefully what is before you; And put a knife to your throat If you are a man given to appetite." (Proverbs 23: 1, 2)

I once was working in road construction. We went to build roads in a rural area. One of our coworkers found wild mangoes and brought them with him. He made the mistake of asking us if we wanted some. He probably had three or four mangoes in hand. It just so happened that at the moment, there was an engineer who used to come from town to inspect our work and he was right there with us.

Here is someone who had a very good salary. He could afford most of the stuff we considered a luxury and out of reach. But without thinking, as we already knew him, he jumped up as a kid of a goat and grabbed the best and biggest two mangoes in this guy's hands. In fact, he snatched them from his hand. We looked at each other with dismay. The gentleman was not bothered at all as he started devouring the mangoes. He did it over and over again, grabbing people's snacks and inviting himself to the meal where he was not welcome. He was a glutton, and it's a shame for a parent to raise someone who cannot control themselves.

Gluttony is the inclination of over-indulgence over food, drink, or wealth. It is sin. When we are full, and we continue eating because the food is good, that is gluttony. It is sin. We must pray for victory over gluttony.

Praying in this sense is for God to deliver those that are already gluttonous and to prevent those of our children who are growing up to never become gluttonous. Now hear me here on two accounts.

Firstly, children do not have manners. They learn as they grow. Do not go name-calling your children because they eat fast or can't stop eating. It is called being a child. But as they grow, teach them to use their tonsils and not smack their mouth, to chew thoroughly, and to stop when they are full but encourage them to ask for more if they are still hungry. No shame about that.

Secondly, we have different eating habits and different stomach capacities. Some people, athletes for instance, can eat the entire chicken whereas others can only eat one thigh. If you can only eat a thigh, do not despise the guy who burns too much energy and needs more of it to replenish his body. This is where Paul's advice kicks in. If you eat or don't eat, let it be for the glory of God. Don't get angry at someone because they can eat more than you can.

Wrath

Wrath or anger is a negative emotion

that is a response to a perceived provocation or threat. Nothing good ever associates itself with wrath.

"For wrath kills a foolish man, And envy slays a simple one." (Job 5: 2)

Job is literally saying that wrath is a form of folly. Now can we get angry? Should we get angry? Of course, it is one of our seven emotions. If we don't express it, we are not humans. Things will frustrate us because they are not going the way we planned, and it will make us mad. I just said it: mad.

There is no beating around the bushes: mad is foolish. When we get angry, we take on a little bit of a foolishness soda. That is why we should get out of it before the sun goes down, lest we be unable to control our actions and sin.

Quoting Psalm 4: 4, Paul says:

"'Be angry, and do not sin.' [And he continues] do not let the sun go down on your wrath, nor give place to the devil.'" (Ephesians 4: 26, 27)

We sin so often by giving place to the devil in our heart and our home…. The devil does not create anything. He cannot impose any emotion to us. We already have those emotions. All he does is to suggest us to take some decisions that will frustrate us and let him sneak into our lives. It is like jumping a rope.

You do not start jumping before the rope wings. You get two people to swing the rope first and you jump in. You start your own wrath and then the devil jumps in if you stay in it for an extended period.

If the devil can use a vehicle to drag us out of God's presence, what should we do? We must destroy that vehicle in prayer. When you pray, pray for victory over wrath, so that when you get angry or one of your folks gets angry, they will not give place to the devil.

Sloth

Read these three great thoughts. The first is from a secular source. "For Satan finds some mischief still for idle hands to do." (Isaac Watts) It is not biblical, but it is full of wisdom. If you stay without doing anything, at least your thoughts will wander away from you and cause sin somehow. The next two thoughts are from the bible.

"Laziness casts one into a deep sleep, And an idle person will suffer hunger." (Proverbs 19:

15)

And

"He who is slothful in his work Is a brother to him who is a great destroyer." (Proverbs 18: 9)

There is no doubt about it. Even society resents lazy people. There will always be something to do if we want to do something. Idleness is rampant in churches. We think there is nothing we can do, or nobody has asked us to do anything, therefore, we do nothing. Solomon is saying that being lazy is just as destroying everything we and others have built. It makes sense.

If you receive five thousand dollars on your tax return for instance and you quit your job because you think you have enough to live on for a couple of months, that is destroying what you've built. Before a month you will have drunk that up, I promise.

When we pray, we must pray that God will help us take the necessary steps to secure our living. Not doing anything is as dangerous as destroying everything. God created us to cultivate the land and subdue it. Work was meant to be a pleasurable activity. It can still be if we find what we are wired to do. That can be another topic. For now, let's see how to use the model of the seven deadly sins in prayer. But first, this model works best for confession circumstances. However, you can use it for any type of prayer.

Practical Prayer

Our father who are in heaven, blessed be your name. Everything you do is perfect.

But the evil man has made his ways crooked. And Father, we have fallen into his trap. We slip into sin every day. But you are good, and your mercies endure forever. That is the only reason we are here to dare to talk to You. Please hear our voice.

Lord, we are proud and have thought of ourselves to be self-dependent. And in our foolishness, we have favored our flesh with the pleasures of this world more than getting closer to You. We have drifted away from You, Lord, and we pray that you will pull us back and give us victory over pride.

Lord, likewise, our greed has caused us to steal your tithes and offerings. We have not been faithful with our worship in giving. Moreover, we have not thought of our brethren even in our prayer. We have wanted to keep all the blessings to ourselves. Please, God, give us victory over greed, so we can become our brother's keeper and the best stewards of the wealth you place in our care.

Our Father, we are lustful and crave for perishable things. Our eyes lust for wealth undivine and our members have not kept the sanctity of your sanctuary. Father, we want to be a living sanctuary, keeping ourselves holy for You.

Let us rejoice with our brother when they rejoice and keep us from envy, covetousness, and hatred. These things are devilish, and you promised an eternal punishment for those who practice them. Please take a hold of our heart, cast out envy from us, and give us victory over it. Since we are stewards of your possessions, Lord of glory, please help us to enjoy what we have with temperance. Let not the devil induce us to overindulge in lustful consumption of our resources as gluttons that have no hope for eternity. Please Father, give us victory over gluttony, for food does not commend us to God.

Father, your word says in James 1: 20 that "...the wrath of man does not produce the righteousness of God." Help us Lord, to not develop a wrath-stricken life, but to educate our emotions to honor the Lord even in stressful situations.

Father, laziness has caused us to leave praying. Even though you advised us, rising early in the morning and sending, to pray without ceasing, so that our path will see your light and that our heart will receive your wisdom, we still don't pray. Please, Father, give us victory over sloth. We ask this in Jesus' name.

You realize I was rushing there. But if you expanded on each of those seven aspects, I trust that the Holy Spirit would help you touch more areas than you can imagine. We are now going to proceed to the normal Christian model of prayer.

THE NORMAL CHRISTIAN MODEL

The model we are about to discuss now is called the normal Christian model because we have observed that most Christians pray following this model. They do it without thinking. It has become a habit. So, if you like it, you are welcome to use it. We are still going to see how to have a systematic method when using this model. This model is a little bit similar to the Lord's model of prayer. But items appear in a slightly different order.

First things first, why would one call this model the normal Christian model? Who is a normal Christian? Why normal? The simple answer is that this model is a default model. When someone has no structured model to follow, they usually default here. So, a normal Christian is just an ordinary Christian. That is you; that is me.

Now let me say something that will sound out of context and maybe counterintuitive for this program. I don't follow the models we are discussing here all the time in the order exposed here. The reason I don't follow them all the time is twofold.

First, public prayer does not need to be too long. If you go over every element I mention here in a public prayer, you are going to be long. It is not necessary to have long prayers in public, to say the least. When Jesus prays for Lazarus His prayer is brief. When He prays for the disciples as He is departing from the world, His prayer is very long, but this is a farewell prayer. In public, be brief and straight to the point. In your personal prayers, you can go for as long as you wish, God loves it.

Second, if we are in a rush, and that will happen, then I'm just going to skip steps. Second, I have developed a good deal of experience praying to the point that the Holy Spirit helps me find my words pretty easily. But this is what I do.

I pray five times a day in a systematic way. Every time I pray on that regular schedule, I follow one model each time. Ideally, I follow the Lord's model the first time I pray by myself, the model of the five areas of life the second time, the model of the seven deadly sins the third time, the model of the normal Christian the fourth time, and the guerrilla model the fifth time.

For the person who would struggle finding their words or who doesn't know where to start, or who just likes structure, or, again, someone who wants to be serious about their prayer, I would suggest using all those models systematically also.

Muslims pray five times a day. Why not us? The Bible says that we should pray without ceasing, and we should. Having five systematic prayers a day would revolutionize our prayer life. Having five 3-minute prayer sessions a day are more important than a one-solid-hour of prayer once a day.

Hear me well. Three minutes times five only gives us fifteen minutes.

$$3 \times 5 = 15$$

But the constant appearance in God's presence

matters. Would you rather your spouse spend one hour in the morning telling you how they love you and forget about you all day long and all night long and come back the next day to do the same thing again, or would you want them to call you regularly and send you texts throughout the day?

Women know this better than we do. They like us to stay in contact. If we like our friend or spouse to stay in contact that much, we must also stay in contact with God.

So, the structure of the normal Christian model usually uses this order: worship or adoration, praise or thanksgiving, confession or repentance, requests or supplications, and final thanksgiving or expression of faith. We will expand on that in a minute but let's briefly go over each item in the list.

Worship or adoration just means recognizing God's lordship or recognizing that only the Lord is God. Praising or thanking God means recognizing His actions in our life. Confessing or repenting means declaring the wrong we have done. Requesting something from God or making supplication or asking a petition means we present our case to Him. Finally, being thankful or expressing our faith is thanking God for what we expect Him to do, accepting it as already done. That's it. Let's now move ahead and do a more thorough dive into each of these items.

Worship

There is a lot of confusion on this term. Some people think that worship is only in slow and soft songs where we are very reverend and respectful. But worship is not as much the outward appearance as the inward attitude.

Worship can be in songs, in giving, in silence, or in words such as prayer. To worship in the biblical understanding is to revere God and to acknowledge that He is God. That means you put Him above everyone else and everything else. It means consecrating oneself to him. In fact, worship is an attitude, a service, an offering.

In his abstract to "Worship principles in the writings of E.G. White," Youngsoo Chung says that "There is no doubt that exegetes, pastors, and church leaders are fascinated by the issue of worship in the Christian church. Carelessness about worship is not an option. In fact, getting worship right has a significant importance because God is at the center of right worship." God dwells in the middle of worship.

101

In Revelations 4: 10 and 11, the Bible says:

"The twenty-four elders fall down before Him who sits on the throne and worship Him who lives forever and ever, and cast their crowns before the throne, saying: 'You are worthy, O Lord, To receive glory and honor and power; For You created all things, And by Your will they exist and were created.'"

This is not just a random occurrence. It has been happening since before the beginning of time. John was fortunate to see it happen. It will never stop. God dwells in worship and in the midst of worshippers. And as you can see in the words of these heavenly elders, worship is the recognition of God's glory, and power, and immense wisdom.

When we pray and worship God, we

must acknowledge these attributes. Not only should we acknowledge and mention them, but we must believe in our heart that God is the only true God. That is what Jesus meant when He said that those who worship God must do it in spirit and in truth.

We must believe that God is the Almighty, the Creator of heaven and earth, and that His glory surpasses all understanding. It is okay to pray just to worship God. It is impressive that most of our prayers are supplications because we need or want something.

How different our lives would be if we spent time every day worshipping God!

Three wise men came from what the Jews called a heathen land to worship the Christ when He was born.

"Where is He who has been born King of the Jews? [They inquired] For we have seen His star in the East and have come to worship Him." (Matthew 2: 2)

And what did these magi bring with them? Costly gifts to partake of the baby shower of the Son of God. Now you will tell me that they were rich and could afford rich gifts, but there is always a costly gift in our disposal that we can bring to God in worship. And I'm not just talking about our heart. It is easy to talk about our heart which we give to God, but if we cannot find anything else but our heart to bring, it must be an exception and not the new norm. Yes, God wants obedience more than the fat of the bulls, but no true worshipper of God has ever been rebuked by God because he or she has brought gifts to the Lord.

When we come to God just to worship Him, we go back with much more fulfillment than when we just come to Him to ask for a service. So, in your prayers, take time to just contemplate your God. Worship is when our attention is on God alone.

Praise

Praise is confused with worship in some Christian churches and literature. Worship is to acknowledge and tell God that He is God. Praise is telling God what He did for us or for someone we know.

Worship is saying, "God, I know you are God, the only one." Praise is saying, "God, I know that you did this for me or for someone I know: thank you for doing that." Get it?

"And she conceived again and bore a son,

and said, 'Now I will praise the Lord.' Therefore she called his name Judah. Then she stopped bearing." (Genesis 29: 35.)

This is Leah talking. She was given to Jacob to wife by trickery. And Jacob didn't love her much. But she was the only wife bearing children at this time. Judah is her forth son, and she says, "*I will praise the Lord*" or I will thank the Lord for what He has done for me. That is praising.

When you pray for something and God gives it to you, you come before Him and say, "Thank you" that means you came to praise Him. All the six verses of Psalm 150 are constructed around praise.

"Praise the   Lord! Praise God   in   His sanctuary; Praise Him   in   His   mighty firmament! Praise Him   for   His   mighty

acts; Praise Him   according   to   His   excellent greatness! Praise Him   with   the   sound   of   the trumpet; Praise Him with the lute and harp! ..."

God's acts are mighty. Whether we know it or not, it takes mighty acts for us to be saved, to wake up in the morning, to eat solid food and build the fabric of our body with that food. That is why we must praise God without ceasing.

When we praise God in our prayer, we must remember to tell Him what He has done for us. We must thank Him for anything we take for granted. There is no such thing as granted.

I once lost my ability to speak and swallow because of cancer. When you come to this point, that's where you appreciate those things we do without thinking. When we wake up in the morning, we must thank God wholeheartedly. When we get a child, when we get a job, when we get a house, a car, a degree. It takes God's mighty acts for us to have those things, and we should confess every time we have concealed God's love in our life. Praise is focusing on what God has done to us.

Confession

Confession is admitting one's wrongdoing. Plainly said, when we confess our sins, we admit in God's court that we are guilty. We plead guilty to the charges of sin. Now here is a trick: it is better for us to plead guilty in the court of God while we are still alive in this earth than to admit it in the heavenly court after this life. That way, our defense attorney in the person of Jesus Christ of Nazareth will step in because He had already redeemed us. We will be released, and the case dismissed. If we die without giving the Lord the permission to defend us in the last day, then whether we plead guilty or not, it will be too late.

Confession is an act of acknowledgment of Jesus's sacrifice for our lives and promoting our faith in Him. Confession must be truthful and remorseful. Pharaoh confessed his sin several times to Moses. But when Moses turned his back and the plague stayed, Pharaoh went back to his stubbornness. This type of confession is not truthful, and no one can fool God with it. He knows that our confession is because we fear the consequences of our sin, not an understanding that sin will separate us from God.

God does not compel anyone to love

Him. If we come to Him because we fear Him, He cannot accept us. But when we come to Him because we love Him, the Lord accepts us and forgives our sin. David was willing to die in the hands of God. He did not plead for the consequences of sin to be removed. He knew he deserved them. Only he didn't want to be separated from God.

Every time we come to God, we must reaffirm our decision to lay our burden on His shoulders. The burden of sin is too heavy for us to bear. Jesus said that we should come to Him and take His yoke upon us.

"Come to Me, all you who labor and are heavy laden, and I will give you rest. Take My yoke upon you and learn from Me, for I am gentle and lowly in heart, and you will find rest for your souls. For My yoke is easy and My burden is light." (Matthew 11: 28-30)

We must confess our sins to God for many reasons. The first is to be clean and not be consumed by God's holiness. No sinner can approach God without first donning the pure garment of grace in Christ.

Let's hear this account.

"In the year that King Uzziah died, I saw the Lord sitting on a throne, high and lifted up, and the train of His robe filled the temple. Above it stood seraphim; each one had six wings: with two he covered his face, with two he covered his feet, and with two he flew. And one cried to another and said: 'Holy, holy, holy is the Lord of hosts; The whole earth is full of His glory!' And the posts of the door were shaken by the voice of him who cried out, and the house was filled with smoke. So I said: 'Woe is me, for I am undone! Because I am a man of unclean lips, And I dwell in the midst of a people

of unclean lips; For my eyes have seen the King,
The Lord of hosts.'" (Isaiah 6: 1-5)

We cannot approach God in our sinful
nature. When you continue reading this
passage of Isaiah, a seraphim flew to him and
purified his lips, so that he could live.

God is so pure that even angels standing
before Him find it impossible to behold Him.
They cover their faces with two wings. That's
how bright God's purity is.

"Can a mortal be more righteous than God?
Can a man be more pure than his Maker? If He puts
no trust in His servants, If He charges His angels
with error, How much more those who dwell in
houses of clay, Whose foundation is in the dust,
Who are crushed before a moth?" (Job 4: 17-19)

Even angels are found lacking before
God. Our sins would not allow us to stand that
kind of purity. It is in Christ Jesus that we have

the privilege to be purified well enough to be able to stand God's presence. But that purification does not take place before we ask for it. We ask for it by confessing.

The second reason we must confess our sins when we come to God is to give Him permission to accept us, so that we can understand His reply to our prayer. Our sins block our attention to God's communication, and it becomes difficult to understand God's response when we are overwhelmed with sinful noise.

Requests

"Now we know that God does not hear sinners; but if anyone is a worshiper of God and does His will, He hears him." (John 9: 31)

This statement can be very misleading.

113

I'm not going to try any exegetic exercise with it though. But, this was someone's statement who barely knew the Lord. He was blind, Jesus had opened his eyes, but he didn't even know Jesus. He is now in front of the religious leaders of his country.

These leaders hate Jesus and have threatened to put out of the synagogue everyone who confesses Jesus as the Messiah. This man was born blind. Jesus just gave him his sight back. He does not know much about Him, and he must defend his case. He makes this statement contained in John 9: 31 above.

We can agree that this man was touched by the Holy Spirit because this statement is illuminating. But taking his statement (in its singleness) for it just because it is in the Bible can be misleading. Now, am I saying his statement is not true? No. But it does not give us the full extent of the revelation. There is, however, a statement coming from someone who knew the Lord very well and was a leader in the church. His name is Peter.

1 Peter 3: 12. *"For the eyes of the Lord are on the righteous, And His ears are open to their prayers; But the face of the Lord is against those who do evil."*

Notice well what Peter is saying. He classifies people in two groups. He starts by calling the one group *the righteous* and the other group *those who do evil.* Now we know that we are all sinners. The righteous here cannot be counted righteous by themselves. There's got to be grace in their lives. For by grace one is saved through faith. Paul clarifies that,

"if you confess with your mouth the Lord

Jesus and believe in your heart that God has raised Him from the dead, you will be saved. 10 For with the heart one believes unto righteousness, and with the mouth confession is made unto salvation. 11 For the Scripture says, 'Whoever believes on Him will not be put to shame.'" (Romans 10: 9-11)

If you have this simple principle, you will be saved. You are a redeemed sinner. You must answer "yes" to the next two questions. Sinner? Yes! Redeemed? Yes! If you answered positively and Jesus can answer positively for you on these two accounts, then you are counted righteous in the Kingdom of God, and God has His ears open to your prayers. Jesus calls you sheep. It does not mean that you do not commit any more sins. It means your sins are not intentional anymore and when you <u>accidentally</u> happen to commit any, you truly repent and turn away from it.

On the other side of the isle are those who do evil. These practice it as their way of life. If someone does evil, that means they have decided to sell their heart to evil. They don't need God; they don't want God interfering in their business. They may claim to be God's, but are promoting the notion that they are humans and can't be without sin. This is the guy God does not hear, unless he gives God permission to work with him by repenting honestly through Christ. Jesus calls him goat.

So, when we pray, we must pray for our heart to not practice evil. We must pray for our family as Job used to do. We must pray for the people around us, in church and in our extended family. If we see someone being in misalignment with the church's tenets, we must pray for them and pray with them if they allow us, instead of gossiping about them.

No one is immune to evil. A little slumber, a little negligence of prayer and other spiritual exercises and our heart will be exposed to evil. The agencies of Satan are in an unending search for the Christians who miss their interview with the Most-High through prayer. The heavenly beings glance at us pityingly as we pass our opportunity to seal our victory against the angel of deception many a time in a single day. Therefore, we must request God's help for our lack of persistence in prayer all the time.

Praying for our own issues is called requests or supplications. Somehow, we can make supplications for others too. Praying for someone else is called interceding. We intercede on someone else's behalf. Both should become our daily practice as there are utmost inevitable blessings to be bestowed upon us when we pray for others.

"*It is more blessed to give than to receive.*" (Acts 20: 35)

There is something in the life of Job that has always championed my faith. Job 42: 10

"*And the Lord restored Job's losses when he prayed for his friends.*"

Not before. Think about that. God had already cleared Job. He could've just restored Job then. But He took Job to a journey where the man Job would learn a lesson that applies to all generations. Job was to partake of his own blessing and minister unto others. Job could barely sleep. But God still taught him to pray for his friends.

God is acquainted with our sorrows. He wants us to take no excuse for skipping prayer.

119

He also teaches us self-denial. Even in unbearable trial and dire losses, God still wants us to intercede for our friends. Job did it. Jesus did it. Stephen did it. We must do it if we will enter our blessings. I hope this lesson revolutionizes your prayer life. Let's make a shift here to see a rather peculiar way a giant in the faith interceded for a people.

Abraham's Intercession

The scene is taking place in Genesis 18. God is about to overthrow two wicked cities: Sodom and Gomorrah. Lot, Abraham's nephew happens to sojourns in Sodom, one of the two soon-to-be-destroyed cities. Let's see the story.

"Then the men turned away from there and went toward Sodom, but Abraham still stood before the Lord. 23 And Abraham came near and

said, 'Would You also destroy the righteous with the wicked? 24 Suppose there were fifty righteous within the city; would You also destroy the place and not spare it for the fifty righteous that were in it? 25 Far be it from You to do such a thing as this, to slay the righteous with the wicked, so that the righteous should be as the wicked; far be it from You! Shall not the Judge of all the earth do right?'*

26 So the Lord said, 'If I find in Sodom fifty righteous within the city, then I will spare all the place for their sakes.'" (Genesis 18: 22-26)

The story is told that Abraham sees three sojourners passing by and runs to them and greets them. He bows down (as the formal polite greeting of the Eastern world was back then) begging them to eat a morsel at his place. After his hospitality, the three men leave Abraham. Among the three is God in bodily form. He remembers Abraham and decides to

121

inform him of the action He is about to take concerning Sodom and Gomorrah.

Abraham is grieved because his nephew, Lot, lives there. The conversation goes on, and Abraham goes from forty to 10 righteous. God repeats the same promise that the city would be spared if there were 10 righteous in it. Here Abraham was almost confident that the life of Lot would be spared.

Why is this an intercession? Abraham was not asking these questions for his own sake. He was asking them to entice God to spare the lives of the righteous in the doomed city. When we pray for someone else, it is called intercession. This intercession has very special lessons.

First, Abraham is interacting with God. He speaks, and he listens. It is not because we cannot see God in bodily form that we must not listen to Him. Prayer is a conversation.

Second, Abraham adjusts his requests. It is okay to go back before God and adjust our requests. That is not a lack of faith. In fact, it shows great faith because we trust God. God does not lie. We are not going back to God with the same request because we want God to change His mind. Instead, we go back to Him to seek a more specific guidance on the response we have received.

Third, Abraham does not pray for the unrighteous. Not surprising. Jesus said, "I do not pray for the world" (John 17: 9.) Does that mean that we should not pray for the unrighteous? In this passage, there was no more time for the unrighteous. God was not going to wait any longer. His decision was made. Abraham did not pray for God to change His decision but to remember the righteous. God will punish this world, but He will remember the righteous.

The time is now to pray for the unrighteous and present them Christ. The only prayer we must pray for the unrighteous is for them to repent. If someone comes to you asking for prayer, you cannot just rush before God to pray for them without them opening their case to you fully. God will not hear you if the person you're praying for is in an open rebellion against God. If they don't want to commit their life to God, we are not to pray for them. If we pray for them, we are wasting our time, and we are tempting God.

What if you are in an outreach program and you find sick people? Even when you visit a hospital, you must get the sick's okay to pray for them or someone who has that authority

124

must let you. If the sick person can speak, you must ask if they believe that Jesus is the Son of God and that God raised Him from the dead. If they don't, there is no reason to pray for them. If they answer you wittingly because they want your blessing, then at least you have their okay. It is their problem with God not yours.

To round up this subject, request means focusing on human's issues and bringing them to God. When God answers us, we must follow with thanksgiving.

Thanksgivings or praises

The Bible says:

"*In everything give thanks; for this is the will of God in Christ Jesus for you.*" (1 Thessalonians 5: 18)

"Thank you" is not only good for your friend. It is spiritual maturity to say thank you to God. He gives us everything. He gives us His oxygen; we drink His water; we live in His world. Forget about those that pretend to own this world. It belongs to God. He owns it all.

Paul says that we should thank God in everything. Now when he says that this is the will of God for us, we might be fast to conclude that God is pleased with our suffering. That's not true.

Going back to Job, this is a just man suffering terrible persecutions. He lived through this, recovered from it, and went his way without a clue of what had happened to him. God showed Moses long after Job was dead what really happened. We know what had happened to Job today because we read it in the book. And when it is presented in the

Bible, we understand that God does not allow Satan to destroy us. He can only try us. So, no matter what you go through, just know that God has taken the insupportable part and let the slightest part to be given to you. The devil's plan is to destroy us completely. God tames down the devil's trials before they reach us.

Now, I know what you might be thinking. People usually ask about the difference between thanksgiving and praise. Simply put, thanksgiving is saying thank you to God for what He has given us or done for us. Praising God is to thank Him at a higher level, such as the dying on the cross for us. But more importantly, being thankful in this context here is the ending of our prayer. This is where we say, "God thank you for what you are going to do."

When we pray, we have the assurance

that God hears us. Not only does He hear us, but He is going to answer us, which is why we thank Him. We anticipate His answer by faith.

Now that we have gone over all the components of a normal Christian model, let's put it in a typical prayer.

Practical Prayer

God of Abraham, God of Isaac, and God of Jacob, my God: Let your name be glorified, and let Your name be exalted because You are God. There is no other god beside You. In You there is life, and life is the light of men. I glorify Your mighty name, Lord. You are the Creator of heaven and earth and everything therein. You are the Alpha and the Omega, the beginning and the end. In Your hand there is power to save and to condemn. I am in front of you right now, Lord.

Lord God, only You can provide for us. I prayed to you once for brother Denzel, and he just found a job. Thank you, Father because you hear us. Your word is true. It says in 1 John 5: 14 that "Now this is the confidence that we have in Him, that if we ask anything according to His will, He hears us." Yes, You hear us, Lord, which is why I put my trust in You.

Father, I have come to talk to You. But I am not worthy of Your holy presence. Therefore, I have brought my sins to You, oh You who provide the ransom for us. Let the blood of Your son blot out my sins and wash my transgressions away. My wife is also in this cry, Father. She is just as much a sinner as I am, and I'm praying for your servant also. Even our daughter, Marie, who is only three is learning the ways of evil because of our nature. I pray, deliver us from our sinful nature.

Father, I have something I want to ask. My driver's license will expire next week. It is my negligence. I received the renewal notice about two months ago, but I did not act. I am going in tomorrow to renew it. Please prepare the day, so that I will go there tomorrow indeed and early in the morning. Prepare the people that will work there tomorrow to be kind and respectful.

Thank you, Lord for your tender mercies. I believe that You have already worked on my case and that tomorrow will be the accomplishment of Your action. I thank you for taking care of the topics I did not even mention here. You know my needs better than I. Thank you, Father. Glory be to Your name in Jesus' name. Amen.

THE GUERRILLA PRAYER MODEL

First off, please don't be upset that I'm using the term guerrilla for a spiritual exercise. I got the term from the business world. In business, guerrilla marketing, for instance means aggressive marketing. In our context, the guerrilla prayer is when you have a hot potato in your hands.

When you have a burning need in hand, you need quick and emergent divine intervention. There is no time to cut through the red tape. This is an aggressive way of requesting God's attention for your case right now.

Whether you know it or not, we have all made this prayer. When your baby is falling from the bed, you lost control of your vehicle, or you broke your dad's watch and want God to soften the punishment, you pray for immediate divine intervention. That is the prayer we are talking about here.

"And it came to pass in the month of Nisan, in the twentieth year of King Artaxerxes, when wine was before him, that I took the wine and gave it to the king. Now I had never been sad in his presence before. 2 Therefore the king said to me, 'Why is your face sad, since you are not sick? This is nothing but sorrow of heart. So I became dreadfully afraid, 3 and said to the king, 'May the king live forever! Why should my face not be sad, when the city, the place of my fathers' tombs, lies waste, and

its gates are burned with fire?' 4 Then the king said to me, 'What do you request?' So I prayed to the God of heaven." (Nehemiah 2: 2-4)

In times past, the king's cupbearer, as well as every servant of the king that was called to stand before him, was to display gaiety and raptured happiness. If there was found on your face a suspicion of gloominess, even if you had a valid reason for it, you could be put to death. But this day, Nehemiah could not just pretend. Neither would the king.

The king's question was partially a death sentence. If not for God's guerrilla intervention, Nehemiah could've been put to death that same day. The dread in his heart was justified by the breaking of the rule of happiness. In a moment, God soothes the king's heart and he is ready to hear what his servant needs to soothe his.

"What do you request?" the king inquired. The dread was even more encompassing. As a servant of the Most-High God, Nehemiah could not lie that his only desire at that moment was to go to Juda and rebuild the walls of the city. But to tell the king that he wanted to leave his presence was equal to raising his head against the monarch. The servant of God was put to the test of faith.

As you may have anticipated, Nehemiah decided to trust his God. His petition was speedily secured by King Artaxerxes. Nehemiah took time off and was provided with the letters to enroll the compliance of the governors beyond the river to provide for his needs.

When in great distress, trust in and aggressive prayer to the Lord are the best insurance coverages a Christian needs. But rather than just doing the guerrilla prayer in an almost adrenaline-filled mind, we are going to see how to do it in a systematic way.

"In a moment, in the twinkling of an eye, at the last trumpet. For the trumpet will sound, and the dead will be raised incorruptible, and we shall be changed." (1 Corinthians 15: 52.)

Paul receives the revelation that it will take a twinkling of an eye for the Lord to perform the best plastic surgery that will bring the dead back to life and change the living. If you can't see what this has to do with prayer, remember that the same God who will do this changing of bodies is the one who answers our prayers.

It takes Him a twinkling of an eye to intervene in our situation. We must be happy and confident that we have a powerful backup continually.

"And Abraham said, 'My son, God will provide for Himself the lamb for a burnt offering.' So the two of them went together." (Genesis 22: 8)

This is a famous story in the Bible. God asks Abraham to sacrifice his son. He obeys. Right at the moment he lifts up his arm to do so, an angel shows Abraham a ram caught in the bush.

This example is another proof that God understands emergency. He knows how to get us out of desperate situations if we find ourselves in an emergent situation.

Now, guerrilla prayer is not just a prayer we do for something to happen in a second. It can be for something to happen in a second or in a very near future. It is better

136

thought as the prayer we make when facing imminent danger. We see it happen with Esther in Shushan.

"Go, gather all the Jews who are present in Shushan, and fast for me; neither eat nor drink for three days, night or day. My maids and I will fast likewise. And so I will go to the king, which is against the law; and if I perish, I perish!" (Esther 4: 16)

As a parenthesis, God's law is the only immutable law. But Satan in his boastful pride has thought of lifting kingdoms to the presumption of gods. And thus, their laws and promulgations such as those of the Medes and Persians would not change once passed. Whomever broke one law was put to death. While God provides a means for forgiveness of our sins, the representatives of satanic powers substitute their means of reparation by

137

effusing the blood of the law-breaker. But time and again the Lord struck a blow at these demonic promulgations when His children were menaced by angels of hell.

Coming back to Esther, there is imminent danger against the Jews. Haman had just bribed the king to sign a death decree against the Jews. Mordecai informs Esther. Esther knows that death is looming either way she goes. The only person she could turn to was the Lord of lords. Therefore, she publishes a three-day fasting and praying. The result is victory.

Fasting and Praying

Jesus is coming down from the mountain with Peter, John, and James. His other disciples are crowded by by-standers and

138

a dismayed father whose child is tormented by a spirit. The disciples could not cast it out. The by-standers and the spies of the pharisees explode in hissing and boasting that the man Jesus who these disciples are following is indeed a deceiver. Here is a test the disciples could neither evade from nor pass.

Jesus comes and rebukes the spirit. The spirit leaves with a great noise. The disciples are speechless, and so are the throngs of the Lord's persecutors. The disciples have cast impure spirits out of their subjects before this incident. What happened with this one? Matthew 17: 21 and Mark 9: 29 tell us that Jesus answered that it takes prayer and fasting to cast this kind out.

You understand by now that guerrilla prayer is also a prayer of power and vigor. To practice guerrilla prayer, we must include fasting. There are some situations that will not change in our lives unless we fast. When we fast, we cleanse our spiritual canal and consecrate them to God, and we gain spiritual clarity.

When your computer is overloaded, its speed slows down. It doesn't slow down because the connection is not high speed anymore. It slows down because the computer is overloaded. When we clean it up, we will be fascinated by how fast it can run.

Fasting cleanses our carnal body to make the spiritual body more able to receive God's input faster. Fasting makes things fast. Additionally, fasting makes us fall in love with God some more. We learn to know God, to love Him, and we learn to please Him. From time to time, we must surrender ourselves to Christ through fasting.

Does it mean that if we fast everything is going to resolve itself? No. But if we fast, most things that stick in our life will not stay. When you clean up your computer, let's say you format it; viruses will be wiped out along with other programs. When you get your computer back, it will be like new. So, when we fast, our body is reformatted, and spiritual viruses fall off.

"Then I proclaimed a fast there at the river of Ahava, that we might humble ourselves before our God, to seek from Him the right way for us and our little ones and all our possessions." (Ezra 8: 21)

Here is a man who had just asked the king for permission to go and build the city of Jerusalem. He told the king how his God would protect him and the congregation with him. And then he realizes that the way from Babylon to Jerusalem is long and ambushed with ruthless criminals. But he is ashamed to ask for guards because the king might ask him if he didn't trust in his God anymore. So, when they get to the river of Ahava, he proclaims a fast to seek God's favor.

If we are afraid of something, we must take it to God in prayer. Fasting would be even better than ordinary prayers. If we have just told our boss that we don't need what he or she is offering because we trust in the Lord, and something just came up and we can't go back because we are ashamed, let's take it to God in prayer and fasting. Guerrilla prayer is also fasting.

I know, most people don't fast nowadays. But nothing must prevent us from fasting. You do not have to go for three days, day and night without food and water. You can skip your breakfast when you first start.

Take it slow and speed up as you become familiar with the practice. I can coach you on this if you decide to learn the practice of fasting.

The Use of Symbolic Elements

The Bible is full of illustrations where a man of God used an element of nature to solve a problem.

"But as one was cutting down a tree, the iron ax head fell into the water; and he cried out and said, 'Alas, master! For it was borrowed.' So the man of God said, 'Where did it fall?' And he showed him the place. So he cut off a stick, and threw it in there; and he made the iron float. Therefore he said, 'Pick it up for yourself.' So he reached out his hand and took it." (2 Kings 6: 5-7)

Elisha is with the sons of the prophets to

cut wood, and one of them accidently drops the ax head into the water. Elisha throws a stick after it and the ax head floats out. There is no logical explanation for this incidence because there is none. God made this to happen by a phenomenon that only shows divine power. In His instruction, iron can float. This was an emergency and needed a guerrilla action. Elisha used a natural element to perform the miracle.

Sometimes, we will be impressed by the Holy Spirit to do something unusual, perhaps out of conventions, but ethical. If we follow the Spirit's impression, we will see God's hand in action. But the instruction must come from the Lord. And we must know how to listen to the voice of the Spirit.

"When He had said these things, He spat on the ground and made clay with the saliva; and He

anointed the eyes of the blind man with the clay."
(John 9: 6)

Jesus is in Bethsaida and a born-blind man seeking for sight is presented to Him. Jesus spits on the ground and makes mud with it. With the mud, He opens the man's eyes. Understandable.

We are made of clay. Jesus, the Creator, makes clay to fix a part in man's body. How appropriate! Once again, the use of natural elements helps resolve a problem. If God Himself uses the elements of nature, it is not bad if the Spirit tells you to do so for a specific case. One of the common elements the church uses is oil.

"Is anyone among you sick? Let him call for the elders of the church, and let them pray over him, anointing him with oil in the name

of the Lord." (James 5: 14)

Oil is the symbol of the Holy Spirit in the Bible. And the Holy Spirit is He who performs miracles in us when we need God's immediate intervention. Using oil in this case is God's recommendation.

Notice that Peter says anointing should be done in the name of the Lord. One day we received the visit of a few brothers and sisters from our church. We started talking about prayer. One sister warmed our hearts with a vivid testimony.

She recounted how I once exhorted the church to pray and ask our petitions in the name of Jesus. She went back that day with a firm resolution to pray in the name of Jesus. As many a Christian before this exhortation, she would just pray saying, "God this God that…

Amen." And this time, she decided to follow my exhortation.

The same week, she asked God for her husband to find a job in Jesus name. The husband found a job the same week. Another day they were traveling when they got a flat tire in the middle of the road. They tried everything to unscrew the tire, but one bolt would not turn loose. They called Triple A (a roadside assistance organization); the guy came with all his gears; the bolt still wouldn't turn loose. And she remembered to ask in Jesus name.

She approached the vehicle where the Triple A guy was toiling unsuccessfully. She started mumbling her prayer to not attract the attention of the guy, and she asked in Jesus name. Right when she'd finished, the key cut on and lo and behold the bolt started turning until completion. And she to exclaim, "This thing works!"

It is heartwarming to hear this kind of testimony of the fidelity of our God. Jesus said,

"If you ask anything in My name, I will do it." (John 14: 14)

The only condition Jesus gave here is that we abide in Him. If what we ask is not going to hurt us or anyone else, if what we ask is going to relieve human suffering, and if what we ask will glorify the Father, Jesus will do it. Peter is therefore correct when he admonishes us to anoint the sick in the name of the Lord because the Lord Jesus will heal the sick.

The elders here are the elders as that applies to our different churches. It also means that a mature Christian can pray for a sick person using oil. In fact, if there is no elder in the vicinity and everybody is a new convert, the Spirit of God still operates in them because the promise of healing the sick is for everyone who believes.

There was no sick person who was not made whole in Israel when Jesus was on earth, save in the villages and towns that did not receive Him. Just think of it for a moment: a city with no sick person because a prophet (as they called Jesus) has healed everyone in the city. How would that city feel? Did you know that Jesus still has the same compassion He had when He was bodily on earth? He still loves us just as equally. He wants to heal us and wants us to pray for healing. What we lack is faith in Christ. And how can we show faith? Just pray for healing! Without presumption, but humbly and with faith. Presumption is to promise healing. If the sick person is okay with that, lay hands on them. God will heal the sick by the laying on of hands.

The laying on of hands

The laying on of hands is a spiritual practice that brings the Holy Spirit into the life of the person on whom the hands are laid. We see it in the Old Testament as well as in the New Testament. In fact, this is a powerful action through which the glory of God operates with might. This action embodies blessing or curse. Now hear me here. By curse, I am referring to the hands that were laid on the sacrificial lamb in the law of Moses.

"And he brought the bull for the sin offering. Then Aaron and his sons laid their hands

on the head of the bull for the sin offering"
(Leviticus 8: 14)

This is the consecration of Aaron and his sons by Moses. The priests' sins are hereby transferred to the bull: that is curse. Sin is curse. On whom the sin falls also falls the curse thereof. That is why Christ is curse for us to be saved. Now there is another form of laying on of hands which is a sign of blessing.

"Then Israel stretched out his right hand and laid it on Ephraim's head, who was the younger, and his left hand on Manasseh's head, guiding his hands knowingly, for Manasseh was the firstborn." (Genesis 48: 14)

This story is the story where Jacob, here called Israel, is bidding his farewell to his family. He blesses the sons of Joseph. His right hand is a sign of authority. He places it on the younger brother and the left hand on the older. By this sign, he predicts that the younger brother, Ephraim, will be more honorable than his older brother, Manasseh. Joseph intervened because it was not in the custom to elevate the younger over the older, but Jacob spoke clearly saying that he did not make a mistake, he did it intentionally.

As you can see, the laying on of hands is a special event. It always brings special manifestations in someone's life. The person with spiritual authority is the one that lays hands on the other to transfer the power of the Holy Spirit over that person for a special manifestation.

A parent can lay hands on their children to bless them or pray for them. A pastor can lay hands on the members of the congregation to bless them, pray for their restoration, or consecrate them to the service of the Lord. The elders can do the same thing in the church. But a child can also lay hands on their parent if they occupy a position of authority or if they implore God's special intervention on their parent's behalf.

If a child has a specific gift, such as the gift of healing as specified in 1 Corinthians 12: 9, he or she can lay hands of their parents. And, if we are praying for someone to heal, we are allowed to lay hands on the person after the person has examined themselves in confession and we have done the same. But we must get permission to do so, or at least inform the person about our intention to lay hands on them. Christ said:

"And these signs will follow those who believe: In My name they will cast out demons; they will speak with new tongues; they will take up

153

serpents; and if they drink anything deadly, it will by no means hurt them; they will lay hands on the sick, and they will recover." (Mark 16: 17, 18)

It is our privilege as believers to lay hands on the sick, so they can recover. Guerrilla prayer also includes laying hands on the person for comfort, blessing, consecration, or recovery. The Lord will intervene.

Class Act

If there is anything corporations don't want to meet in their way, that is a class action lawsuit. Google says that "A 'class action' lawsuit is one in which a group of people with the same or similar injuries caused by the same product or action sue the defendant as a group." Examples of class action lawsuits that have rung the bells in

America include pharmaceutical drugs, dangerous products, or frauds.

One of the biggest class actions is was Dukes vs Wal-Mart Stores. The lawsuit was filed in 2000, seeking a settlement of $11 billion dollars. CBS reports that "A female employee is suing Wal-Mart Stores for sexual discrimination under Title VII of the Civil Rights Act of 1964 claiming that after several years of excellent work evaluations she was denied a promotion. The case was converted to class-action status to represent every female employee from 1998 onwards." As of the putting on file of this material, that settlement hasn't reached the agreement yet. That's how big an issue a class action lawsuit is.

We are wronged by the devil daily. We must sue him daily. More importantly, instead of just going against him for a single case, we must come together in a class action lawsuit. Pastor and Dr. Denton Rhone, Ph.D. says that when we come corporately to pray for a topic, it gets Heaven's attention. Jesus said that where two or three are gathered together He is in their midst. When we need divine direct intervention, it is a good idea to invite friends, family members, and church members to join ventures and prepare a class action lawsuit against the enemy. The first class action must take place in your family. If your family does not pray together it is in permanent danger. That can constitute another course, but you catch my drift.

CONCLUSION

My dear friend, what else could I have said? This is not it. It is the beginning of a great journey, a journey full of surprise and blessings. A journey full of discoveries and lessons to learn. I feel humbled that the Lord used me to help you increase your prayer life, so that you can expose yourself to the Holy Spirit regularly. I advise you to do it.

We studied five models of prayer that will really impact your life and the lives of those around you. Think of the Model of Jesus, the model of the five areas of life, the model of the seven deadly sins, the model of the normal

Christian, and the guerrilla model. Listen to these recordings at least once a month. I trust our Heavenly Father that every time you listen to them, the Holy Spirit will teach you something new, something I didn't even intend to show you because He was the Author of this book and He will be your teacher.

If you need specific help about life or spiritual matters, please reach out to me personally. Send me a message at winningasoulministries@gmail.com. I will be glad to assist. If this program blessed you, please let me know as well. If you want to send a testimonial to help others find it, please do so. You may also share the news to your friends and family members so that they will be blessed also. This is a ministry first. If you have a special need and would want us to help, please let us know. If you want a speaker for your event, please reach out to us.

"The Lord bless you and keep you; The Lord make His face shine upon you, And be gracious to you; The Lord lift up His countenance upon you, And give you peace." In Jesus' name. Amen.

APPENDICES

Use these questions for your discussions.

Appendix A: The Model of Jesus

1. In the Lord's prayer, Jesus starts with the name of the Father. Can you find anywhere else in the Bible where the name of Lord comes first, before any mention of men? Why do you think this is?

2. Can anyone pray the Father or should we rely on our religious leaders to intercede for us?

3. In Exodus 20: 7 the Bible says, "You shall not take the name of the Lord your God in vain." Can you think of any way one can take the name of the Lord in vain?

4. Isaiah 64: 6 says that "all our righteousnesses are like filthy rags." Can we therefore claim to have any right when we come before God for prayer? Please explain.

5. Let one member of the group ask a question concerning this topic and the rest of the group discuss it. If you are studying on your own, think of a question someone who is not familiar with the Bible might ask you about prayer and answer it.

Appendix B: The Model of the Five Areas of Life

1. Discuss the meaning of worshiping God "in spirit and truth."

2. How does sin affect our health?

3. How can we love our neighbor as ourselves? Find some examples of what would be illegitimate to do to our neighbor even though we find it fine to do it to ourselves.

4. Spend time pondering on this statement: "But if anyone does not provide for his own, and especially for those of his household, he has denied the faith and is worse than an unbeliever." (1 Timothy 5: 8)

5. Spend time pondering on this prayer: "I do not pray that You should take them out of the world, but that You should keep them from the evil one." (John 17: 15)

Appendix C: The Model of the Seven Capital Sins

1. As much as you can, find the origin of the expression, "I'm proud of you!" and form two groups. The one should argue that this expression must be banished from the English language. The other will argue against.

2. "Be kindly affectionate to one another with brotherly love, in honor giving preference to one another" (Romans 12: 10) Dissect and discuss about this verse.

3. What are some spiritual and social dangers of dishonest sexual life? Base your answer on the Bible.

4. "For wrath kills a foolish man, And envy slays a simple one." (Job 5: 2) Take two minutes for each member of the group to confess (if applicable) any anger-related sin they have ever manifested and let one person seal it in prayer.

5. "Laziness casts one into a deep sleep, And an idle person will suffer hunger." (Proverbs 19: 15) Without becoming too political, discuss the outcomes of laziness as applied to your country.

Appendix D: The Normal Christian Model

1. Read Revelations 22: 8,9. In this context, what is worship and how should we worship God?

2. Is there anything you want to thank God for today? Please express it before everybody. Now pray to seal your blessings in the blood of Jesus, lest Satan put a hold on them[1].

3. What are some spiritual and social dangers of dishonest sexual life? Base your answer on the Bible.

4. There is only one thing that puts barrier between God and Men. That thing is sin. How can we biblically fight sin in our life? Please be specific.

---

[1] Check my program "How Satan puts a hold on our blessings." If it's not yet available, write to me, and I will email you the unreleased files.

5. "And the Lord restored Job's losses when he prayed for his friends." (Job 42: 10) Ask God of anything you want right now (according to His will.) Write to me if you want me to pray for you.

Appendix E: The Guerrilla Model

1. How necessary do you think fasting is for Christian life?

2. How would you feel if someone were praying for your sickness and made mud with their saliva and was coming to apply it on you? Why do you think Jesus did this?

3. How comfortable are you with the laying on of hands? Why?

4. Do you have a prayer partner? You must have one. Discuss how each of you is going to find a prayer partner.

5. Thank God for the journey you took with me. Please ask Him to keep me safe and more inspired and zealous for His work. Thank you and God bless you.

ABOUT THE AUTHOR

Vitalis Essala put this book to your disposal, so that you can grow spiritually, promote the Kingdom of God, and cast the darkness of this world asunder one family at a time. As an engaged worker in the field of soul-winning, he specializes in prayer and teaching the Word of God. He has pastored churches and managed different ministries in the space of over 20 years. His wife and he founded **Soul Winning Ministries** to equip families in their walk with the Lord. Vitalis is a speaker, teacher of the Word, and intercessor. He is spearheading a wonderful ministry for men called, **Proverbial Men** where men meet together and study to become better husbands and better fathers to their families through the book of Proverbs. Vitalis earned a Bachelor of Science in sociology and organizational leadership from Arizona State University.

OTHER PRODUCTS FROM THE AUTHOR

Books

1. **Act On Your Dream Today**: The Principles of Stability and Human Excellence Part 1 – 2015

2. **The Belief Vaccine**: Identifying, Treating and Curing The Diseases of Self-Doubt – 2016

3. **Mon Seul Péché** (short novel in French) – 2017

4. **How to Listen to God**: 9 Channels you Must Use to Understand God's Will for your Life – 2018

Audio CDs and Downloadables

1. **Take a Sip: It's Self-confidence** – 2018
2. **5 Models of Prayer**: How to Prayer Fervently Well and Expose yourself to the Holy Spirit Constantly – 2018

Online Courses

1. **Building Productivity**: The Netflix Way (Udemy.com) – 2018
2. Practical Guide for Cancer Survivors: Leading a Meaningful Life After Severe Pain (Teachable.com) – 2019.

CONTACT THE AUTHOR

winninagsoulministries@gmail.org

Join us on Facebook: Sharing the Word Group

Made in the USA
Columbia, SC
04 March 2022

57079934R00109